A SHINING FRAGMENT

Doris English

ISIS
LARGE PRINT
Oxford and Orlando

Copyright © Doris English, 1999

First published in Great Britain 1999
by The Book Guild Ltd

Published in Large Print 2000 by ISIS Publishing Ltd,
7 Centremead, Osney Mead, Oxford OX2 0ES, and
ISIS Publishing, PO Box 195758,
Winter Springs, Florida 32719-5758, USA
by arrangement with The Book Guild Ltd

British Library Cataloguing in Publication Data
English, Doris
  A shining fragment. – Large print ed.
  1. English, Doris 2. English, Tom 3. World War, 1939–1945
  4. Large type books 5. Suffolk (England) – Biography
  I. Title
  942.6'4'084'0922

ISBN 0-7531-9611-5 (hb)
ISBN 0-7531-9615-8 (pb)

Printed and bound by Antony Rowe, Chippenham and Reading

A SHINING FRAGMENT

ENGLISH, D.

920 NF

ENG

A shining fragment

This item is to be returned on or before the latest date above.
It may be borrowed for a further period if not in demand .

CONTENTS

PREFACE

A shaft of sunlight between slightly drawn curtains can best describe Tom English's sojourn in Suffolk in 1939. He recognised the signs of the times and was painfully aware of the part he would have to play, including the inevitable ultimate sacrifice. Our meeting marked the beginning of Tom's life as a man with a crusade. Regardless of all obstacles — not least his life in the RAF, in a country on a war footing — he was so sure of his overwhelming love that nothing deterred him from his pursuit of me. Against all difficulties, which to begin with included my own misgivings, he did triumph. Although someone closed those curtains brutally and abruptly, Tom had proved his outstanding qualities of endurance. Today, almost 60 years later, he lives on.

INTRODUCTION

It is early May 1997. There is a new Labour government, elected today, with such a landslide victory that I was immediately reminded of the jubilant scenes accompanying the 1945 Labour election success following the end of World War II. That day as a young woman I had danced along the corridors at the Department of Employment office in Cambridge where I worked. There was a similar feeling of hope and optimism. Then, we had felt that life could only improve following the most devastating previous six years. I refer, of course, to the changes and events that living through that time brought to virtually every living soul in Britain.

I have just recently celebrated my eighty-third birthday. These two events have caused me to reflect upon the amazing changes that my generation has seen. It seems to me that it is the pace of change that is so fascinating today. I have tried to embrace change. I rely on television, use an electric toaster, and love my freezer. But there are limits to how fast I can adapt. I wonder how today's young people will be equipped to cope with the inevitable changes of the twenty-first century. They at least have a head start, already responding well to commercial pressures to acquire the latest mobile phone or other new gadget.

Until World War II came along to dislodge our lives for ever, I lived in an East Anglian community that had not changed in my lifetime. Looking back, it is hard to believe that the quiet and steady life in Haverhill town, Suffolk, just before war, was so dramatically changed for ever by world events.

Life then was comfortable because it was governed by a set of unwritten rules that everyone knew and largely lived by. I felt, for instance, that I experienced a real childhood. We played games endlessly in the street. There was very little traffic to fear. I recall that the main journeys were made by the Gurteen's factory cart taking finished clothing to the station twice a day and farmers transporting grain to the mill. Our house was next door to the mill. How my mother moaned when the air was dust-laden from the milling.

As children, if we used bad language or "rude" words I believe that they were used in all innocence. My impression was that adults were mostly polite towards each other. We truly took time to notice and acknowledge one another in the street. Of course life was slower; we mostly walked, so perhaps conversation was easier than today, when most people are enclosed in cars.

Although life seemed uncomplicated we were no angels. Like many people, I well remember pinching apples. I can also recall taking sweets from the counter whilst the lady assistant, who might be making up an ice cream cornet, had briefly turned her back. It was a kind of game, played in a school holiday when I was about ten years old.

As children, we freqented a magic world made from our imagination. We had few possessions, but I am sure that growing up in the 1920s and 30s was happy in spite of material hardships. There were exciting times such as the annual sheep sale, when drovers who had walked their animals from as far away as Norfolk descended on the town. In true community spirit, folk offered welcome, food and a bed. One local spinster from a farming family became particularly well known as she had room to accommodate several drovers, who gratefully slept on her floor. She provided a splendid breakfast, knowing that for many there was a long walk home with any unsold stock. I remember one evening lying in bed, the window wide open. The air was full of the smell and sound of sheep drowning every sense as it permeated the house.

Today traffic rules the roads and we take our lives in our hands every time we step out of our homes. I remember well how when someone near us was taken very ill, straw was spread across the road to deaden the the sound of passing horses and carts to give the patient some peace. The roads were dusty, particularly in summer. We loved to follow the cart and horse sent laden with casks of water to dampen the roads. It was fun to watch the process and to compete with friends to catch some of the cool water sprays.

It seems remarkable now, but to me that time stood still. I could never have anticipated, or in my wildest imagination dreamed up, the effects that the war was to have on Haverhill, or the direction of my life.

This is to be the story of what happened to me. It is essentially a love story without an end. There are happy moments to recall and humorous events. But the telling has a serious purpose. I am writing for people of today, because I wish to share the experience of tragic loss, my feelings of the futility of conflict and its aftermath. I believe it is the consequences of war that reach further than most of us would care to imagine.

The events that I am about to relate happened nearly 60 years ago and were not looked for by me. My memory is clear. The feelings and emotions were real and seem undiminished by time.

This is a tribute to one young man which aims to keep his hopes alive. And, as events rarely happen in isolation, I will relate how some of the many other influential people in my life were prominent players in the story, all making their unique contribution.

To set the scene, I will try to give you a flavour of life in pre-war Haverhill. The whole nation had been stunned when at the end of 1936 our king, Edward VII, abdicated. The king was held in great affection by us all. He appeared, even to the younger generation, to be a man of the people. During the First World War he had seen action as a second lieutenant in the First Battalion Grenadier Guards. When the great Depression came, we saw that he wanted to learn about his subjects' economic difficulties. He was not afraid to visit depressed areas and talk to families. This resulted in his personal campaigns against unemployment and for housing. He was a champion for ex-servicemen, believing that they should have the recognition and care that they deserved. The king had achieved the love and admiration of a whole nation. Is is interesting to recall just how much the world political map has altered since those days. Our king ruled over many British dominions overseas and was Emperor of India. As young British subjects, we were all brought up with strong sense of Britain's power and influence in the world. Even living in a small town in rural England we felt a great pride in being part of something larger than ourselves. How different the perspective must be for today's young people.

When the abdication was actually announced there had been a feeling of anticipation, particularly in London, where a crowd estimated at 10,000 waited for the news outside Buckingham Palace. It was a shock, the unthinkable had occurred. But a strong loyalty was quickly established for our new king, George VI and his consort. Soon we were all forced to turn our attention to political events in Europe. Already in 1936 there was beginning to be a different feeling to our lives. Military names were given to products.

For example:

Haywards Military Pickle
Makes Sunday's Meat Monday's Treat

For those young enough to be baffled by the slogan, the explanation was that the majority of families ate a large Sunday roast dinner.

"Leftover" meat was served cold with pickle and fried vegetables the next day. Monday was traditionally washday, when cooking was kept to a minimum. Most families had to stretch that Sunday roast far into the following week.

The average wage in 1938 was £3 10s (£3.50) a week. About 10s (50p) would be spent on rent and much of the rest on food. Very few people owned a car or took holidays. Our houses were not centrally heated and even in winter not every room would have a fire. We were taught not to be extravagant. For instance, it was usual to light a room with a 25-watt bulb. To buy a 100-watt bulb was considered quite unnecessary. Luxury items were beyond most people's pocket. A pair of silk stockings would have cost me 6s 10d. This was out of the question. But a modest pleated skirt, suitable for work, cost around 3s. Worn with a blouse and cardigan, it provided an acceptable outfit, if unexciting by today's standards.

A man whose wages were as high as £5 per week was certainly very comfortably off. That level of wage, paid to people like bank managers, enabled the household to employ a "general" to cook, clean and carry out most household chores.

CHAPTER ONE

Life in Haverhill

I have lived in Haverhill all my life, but that was not so for all the family. Whilst my first experiences of work were in junior school teaching and still living at home with my parents, one of my brothers, John, had married Ellen and moved away to live in London at Parsons Green. The couple had what I recall as a lovely big flat with large light windows. It was warm and welcoming. I remember that my sister-in-law was an excellent cook; the details of her menus are hazy and by today's standards would probably have appeared unexciting, but I loved visiting and staying with her.

It was at John's home that the whole family spent Christmas 1938. My parents, two brothers and two sisters were all assembled. We had a turkey sent from Ireland. For a reason that I do not remember, my parents, who normally spent Christmas in Haverhill, had agreed to us all being together at John's flat. We spent a pleasant time but my mother was keen to return home soon after the festivities were over. As my holiday stretched into the new year. I stayed on in London, where I soon learnt to appreciate the thrill of the theatre. This was to be the beginning of a lifelong love. I well remember lying in bed at the close of 1938 and wondering just what 1939 would bring to us all. That occasion was the last time we were ever to be together as a family under one roof. It must have been an experience repeated all over Europe, for a year later England was to be nearly four months into World War II. The war separated us cruelly in the directions that our lives took and the losses most families suffered.

It is easy to think that because the date when Britain declared war on Germany is so precise, that it was a case of no war one day and then suddenly on 3 September 1939, there was a war. Preparations, rumours and a climate of dedicated nationalism were rumbling on throughout 1938 and 1939. But we knew that the government was preparing for conflict. I read in the newspapers, for instance, that £10 million was spent in 1938 to keep the navy on a "war footing". An estimated £13 million was put into Air Raid Precaution (ARP) provision. Nearly £3 million was spent on sandbags and fire-fighting equipment. Millions were spent on making commercial premises safer against attack. The Auxiliary Air Force was "called up" to serve their country, mainly to operate anti-aircraft units and organise the women's territorials. Everyone, including children, was issued with a gas mask, at the cost of 2s 6d each. By the summer of 1939, when conflict seemed imminent, Anderson shelters were being erected in back gardens. They were made from sheets of corrugated metal, bent to form a shelter. The whole structure was then banked up with earth and was considered adequate to protect us from the effects of bombing raids.

We were encouraged to grow vegetables via a national "Dig for Victory" campaign. The culture of saving items became endemic. Huge piles of scrap metal were collected, mainly by children. It was intended for aircraft manufacture but little was ever used. We all collected glass, rags, newspaper and saved bones. Knitting became popular, with boys and girls being encouraged. Somehow we believed that all these noble efforts would save us from war. No doubt the politicians had a different viewpoint.

Even though all the signs were there, we somehow believed that our government would be able to avoid Britain being drawn into the mounting conflict in Europe. The London Bakers, who set prices for bread, announced that the price of a large loaf of bread in 1938 (8d) would be maintained. (A small loaf was obtainable for around 2 1/2d). A spokesman said, "We desire to make a national gesture of confidence in the outcome of the Prime Minister's efforts for peace." They should have stuck to their trade — at least they were successful!

Entertainment opportunities were relatively limited in Haverhill but we were content. There was a cinema for family use. Most people went to see a film each week. It cost around 4d for a seat and, armed with a 1d bar of chocolate to eat, provided many happy afternoons for me and my friends. There were pubs, of course, but they were definitely male territory. There were regular dances at the Town Hall on Saturday nights. I belonged to the dramatic society in my early twenties and my friends there encouraged me to join them for these nights out. Quite honestly, I did not really relish the evenings. Peer pressure must have been a factor. Many of my contemporaries became quite excited at the prospect of meeting a young man at a dance. I really preferred reading, walking or the cinema, but most young people are carried along by the crowd.

In 1938 there was an added excitement provided by the young airmen who were now stationed at the many bases around East Anglia. Those at Stradishall would be bussed into Haverhill on Saturday nights, where they began the evening drinking and smoking, usually at the Bell Hotel, which still exists today. The camps did arrange dances but it was certainly not acceptable for respectable young women like myself to attend them. The lads were all away from home and were thrown together to live in company they may not have chosen. There was a wariness from our community, particularly from my parents' generation. The airmen were seen as our invaders, a force that unsettled our cosy existence. Individually, of course, they were just like us, but the public face of the airmen was of a drunken or bawdy Saturday night display in our quiet town. No doubt the local publicans were delighted at the increase in trade and the men gave us plenty to discuss, especially as inevitably relationships began to develop between us and them.

It was at one of the Town Hall dances that this story really begins.

My life was comfortable and settled. I enjoyed my work and took great delight in taking long walks with friends. My particular friend, Marion Castle, who was also a teacher, and I were in the habit of walking together through the surrounding countryside, enjoying that weekend feeling of

5

freedom as we discussed books, plays and life. There was a kind of quiet contentment about existence. I certainly did not want anything or anyone to disrupt it.

On the last Saturday in March 1939 we had taken our usual walk. It had been very cold and spring was only just showing itself. I remember being so relieved to sit by the fire at home late in the afternoon, eventually feeling warm and comfortable again. My heart sank a little when I realised this cosy state was temporary, for much against my real wishes I had agreed to support that evening's dance at the Town Hall. It was a fund-raising event for the evening institute, where I readily attended evening classes. It would have been churlish not to have gone that evening. My attitude was more one of duty than expectation of enjoyment. Most of my contemporaries seemed to relish these occasions but I felt uncomfortable, unable to relax. Nevertheless that evening, which was to change my life, stands out in my memory.

The Town Hall, a fine building built with funds provided by the Gurteens, hosted these events admirably. There was a stage for the band at one end, a room where refreshments, usually coffee and cakes, were sold, and down each side a long shiny wooden bench. It seems amusing now but the young men and women really did sit on opposite sides. That particular evening the hall was crowded; it was an impressive turnout. By soon after 10 p.m. I was feeling tired and ready to go home. I had spent the evening pleasantly chatting with friends and watching others dancing. I knew how to dance well enough, but I cannot say it was my passion in life to do so.

The atmosphere was light-hearted, thick with smoke and youthful laughter. For some reason I turned away from the group, my attention probably alerted by the RAF men who had just arrived. Their presence as outsiders was obvious by the deep tones of their joking together and their having all too clearly walked from the Bell Hotel opposite the church. This venue, I knew, would have been the main focus of their evening. It was known that these young men remained in the town until their midnight bus took them back to the base at Stradishall. They obviously had time to fill in. So, often with beer as their courage, they would visit the Town Hall events.

As I turned I was immediately aware that one young airman was looking straight at me. He behaved as if he knew me already but that I was the last person he had expected to see looking back at him. It was a defining moment. I was both intrigued and slightly disturbed. His intense expression filled my consciousness. His gaze did

7

not diminish as he shyly but firmly asked me to dance. It was immediately obvious that he was not an accomplished dancer. He did not even introduce himself. We danced — a polite and rather cool experience outwardly. But in those few moments we were changed for ever. My companions called across the hall to me, by name. So, making my excuses as politely as possible, I turned to leave.

As we parted that first evening he touched my hand with an unexpected lightness and sensitivity. He spoke in earnest with complete conviction.

"I have met you just in time and I shall not let you go." This statement struck me to the core of my being. I felt that he meant it, but a deep foreboding accompanied my thoughts, both emotions residing uncomfortably together. A stranger had held me in his arms, expressed sentiment and promise that I hardly knew how to accept; in an instant turned my life inside out. I made a hasty departure with my friends.

I spent a sleepless night. The next day I was pale and tired; my family commented on my obvious distraction. Laughing it off as mere fatigue, I secretly felt that perhaps the previous evening's experience was written all over my face. Disguising my feelings outwardly did present a problem, but this was not an experience that I was ready or willing to share with my parents.

Sunday passed without incident.

The usual Monday routine at school completely absorbed my energies and attention. In the evening I attended a craft class at the institute. In that situation my thoughts were mine and naturally came back to Saturday evening's events. There would have been much chatter amongst us all about the band, moneys raised and general discussion. My few minutes' encounter with a stranger began to seem unreal. Imagine my surprise when the headmaster brought me a letter. It was simply addressed to "Miss Doris at the evening institute." My friends calling me had told him my name and my nervous chatter about the reason for the dance told him the rest.

I managed to wait until retiring to the privacy of my room that night before reading the note. It was short and to the point.

RAF Stradishall.

Dear Doris,
    I danced with you on Saturday night.
    Would you meet me one evening?
    I wait with impatience to hear from you telling me place and time.

        Sincerely,
            Tom English

CHAPTER
TWO

First Date

You can imagine my mixed emotions at receiving Tom's letter. I did not realise at the time but it was an occasion for mental debate, making up my own mind about a situation. It was a predominant view that "decent girls" did not go out with airmen. It was certainly not acceptable for a young woman in respectable employment, from a well-known family, to actually go to dances at the air base. I sensed the weight of parental disapproval. Yet Tom's letter seemed reasonable. The decision to meet would be mine. I could name the time, date and place. The more the conflicting reactions churned in my mind the more indecisive I felt. I slept on it.

Tom had made an impact. I too had the feeling of discovering something precious. And as nurture preserves the precious, I was not surprised to find I had written and posted my reply before doubt changed my mind.

We met the following Saturday at 7 p.m. under the school clock tower. My dress was simple, a blue pleated skirt, oatmeal sweater and jacket. Spring was on its way. Our formal introduction was nervous. But I learned quickly that Tom loved the countryside and walking, so at my suggestion we set off for a much loved landmark oak tree at Withersfield. It was reassuring to discover that we shared a love of nature and that drinking and dancing were truly not to either of our tastes. Tom told me about his home in Northumberland and how he missed the hills and his family, especially his beloved mother. He was out of uniform, explaining that to him it represented duty and work, all of which he took seriously. But he needed his own identity.

I was puzzled, asking him why he had joined the RAF. He seemed troubled by something.

We soon arrived at the tree, which stands today. We climbed the grassy bank nearby and sat together on the top bar of a wooden stile. It was a perfect evening. A last blackbird sang to us from deep in the hawthorn hedge bordering the meadow that was our view. Tom was quiet, thoughtful.

He wore a badge in his lapel. I wanted to know more so I asked to see it. I studied the bat image and read the motto out loud, "Into the Night we Fly."

Quietly, Tom explained that he was a wireless operator in a bomber and that at present he was involved in training flights in Wellington aircraft.

I knew there was more, which reluctantly he explained. He told me without emotion that they were to be ready in the event of war. Also, if attacked he would have to retaliate, climbing into the Wellington's tail to operate the rear guns.

I was shocked. To actually be talking to a man training to kill others was completely outside my experience. I could not comprehend it. We knew there was a danger of war, but at that time we in rural England felt it very unlikely to happen. There was a confidence that the politicians would be able to resolve the rumbling problems in Europe.

Tom, however, made me think again. He was serious. What he was telling me was real. There was a deep sadness in his eyes that betrayed his true feelings. At that moment I both hoped he was wrong about war and felt slightly foolish and overprotected by my lifestyle.

I could tell that he felt we had reached some level of understanding. I sensed that he was racing ahead, wanting more intimacy. But Tom's sensitivity must have told him that I had made as much progress as possible at that point. He suggested we make our way back. It was getting dark.

"Doris — look at me." Tom's voice was pleading.

I faced him and noticed clearly for the first time how remarkable he was, with his fine hazel eyes, a determined chin and light brown, crisp, wavy hair.

He went on, "Do you feel something special about us? Please forget it's the first time we've walked and talked together." He paused. "I have been waiting for you all my life."

Raising an eyebrow I asked, "And how many times have you said that in your travels?"

He took hold of my hands and said very seriously, "I'm not playing games with you, Doris. There is no time for games. I dare not waste a precious moment now that I have met you."

Unable to look into his eyes, I turned from him. "I just cannot believe you can be so sure." Then turning back to him I challenged, "You can't possibly know who you've been waiting for."

Gently raising my chin to meet his gaze, he asked, "Do you know what your feelings are?" He gave me a searching look.

"I'm confused, Tom. I've never met anyone like you."

He took hold of my arm. "And I've never met anyone like you, Doris, but I'm not confused. I know what I feel." His voice became more insistent. "Please. Don't doubt my sincerity because of your uncertainties. Don't turn away from me. Look at me! Do you remember what I said to you just as we finished dancing? Do you?"

Startled by his urgency, I faltered a little. "Well . . . yes. Yes, I think so. You said: 'I've met you in time', or something like that and, well, I thought you might have had too much to drink. You said you hadn't come to the dance until after The Bell had closed! However, when I thought about it later, I was disturbed."

"Go on." His eyes never left my face.

"Well, then I remember thinking you didn't know where I lived, so I was — safe." There was a short silence. "'Safe' — now why did I use that word, I wonder?" I put my hand over my eyes. "Wait a minute, Tom. I can see why I felt that way. You know — in plays. Priestley does it when something significant has been said, 'a clock chimes'. That's exactly how I felt — as if a clock had struck!"

Tom opened his mouth to speak, but I hurried on. "I was disturbed because you had made an impact on me and I suppose I didn't want to face the possibilities." Anxious now, I asked, "Have I made sense to you, Tom? I've tried to be honest." A look of wonderment crossed his face and his hand slipped down into mine. "So perhaps," I said gravely, "I can agree there is something special about us. Don't try to give it a name just now, though."

14

We walked hand in hand, chatting comfortably, talking of our likes and dislikes. Tom liked the cinema. Dancing he hated. Why did he go to dances? Somewhere to go until the bus took them back to camp. Did he read? Not much, but he wanted to now he had met me. Why? Because I was opening a new world for him.

As we parted, he asked, "When can I see you again? Monday? Tuesday . . .?"

I paused for a moment. "Next Saturday. Here at the same time."

"Why? Why another week before I see you again, Doris?"

"I must have time to think, Tom. Nothing like this has happened to me before. I must be sure."

"Very well. I'll be here."

He seemed disappointed at my reluctance. He nevertheless accepted it, for he knew I had no idea of the world in which he was living and his urgency must seem uncalled for, bordering on the ridiculous.

In the light of the street lamp I saw the look on his face. Sad, tender, rather like a father looking at a child. Unable to meet that look, I wished him goodnight.

I walked away and did not look back.

CHAPTER
THREE

Easter 1939

I was in turmoil. My life, which until meeting Tom had moved along in a comfortable if predictable way, had been thrown into the air. I wondered if I could ever return to the days before Tom.

Tom clearly found our situation difficult. He had such an unshakeable belief in us as a couple and yet had to experience all the frustration of conflicting loyalties. His sense of duty was admirable but he both missed his home and, I came to understand, also felt trapped in a life he would not have chosen. So many of our young men, full of hope and energy, were in the same position. It certainly was not fair that they were called to devote their lives to defending the country, because as individuals they were not responsible for the political situation in Europe. But the sense of duty and pride with which our young fighters conducted themselves should never be forgotten. So many were doomed to an early death. So many families suffered. Still today there cannot be a family in this country that was untouched by the consequences of war. I think we were right to believe it would not actually happen, because the alternatives were too bleak to contemplate. Our parents, who had lived through the First World War, also prayed that another war could be avoided. I can only conclude that we are warlike as a species; history confirms that devastating thought.

So, it must have been frustrating for Tom to spend the whole week following our first date simply waiting for the following Saturday evening. We had agreed to the same time and place. I was a little late. Poor Tom. He admitted his fear that I would not appear. I could see the relief in his eyes as we met, tempered by the anxiety a week's parting had produced.

We quickly re-established our rapport. Soon we were walking, laughing, talking, exchanging comments about the countryside emerging into the beautiful spring.

Tom clearly had something on his mind, an idea — he was effervescent.

We were sitting on a gate impressing each other with our knowledge of crops. I told him how the winter barley should have been high enough to cover a hare but was late this year. I may have been nervous, talking too much to disguise both my excitement and uncertainties.

Tom soon became more direct. "What are you doing next weekend? It's Easter and we can have days together. Where would you like . . .?" The words tumbled out with enthusiasm.

I felt his shiver of disappointment as quietly I broke the news that there were already arrangements for me to stay with my brother John and his wife in London. He protested, but quickly sensed my resolve. For me it was an opportunity to express the fears already growing inside.

I climbed down from the gate and moved closer to him. The last thing I wanted to do was cause pain, but it was time to express my feelings. I told him as gently as possible that for me to become involved with him was unwise. He could be posted away at any time, but I also had to admit that I also did not want that to happen. I was realising that the strong emotions developing between us were a powerful force.

Tom was more expressive. "Doris," he reassured me "don't you know yet that wherever I am, whenever I go away, I cannot forget you?" More urgently, he implored, "I have no life without you."

Tom was so sure of his feelings that, despite my inability or unwillingness to agree, those powerful words told me he also had great patience. He would wait for me to catch up.

My emotions were in turmoil as we parted that evening. The courage to change my Easter arrangements was not there. Self-doubt and sadness at our parting, led to a tearful goodbye. But I managed to give Tom my brother's address and, with the promise of a letter, he left me, probably, poor man, with a heavy heart.

The bus journey taking me from the world of Suffolk to the much wider one of London gave me time to consider the turn my life was taking. Tom. Everything led to him; was influenced by him — my thoughts and actions. Already I was missing him. For the first time a visit to my brother lost its appeal. But I was sure that I was doing the sensible thing; it would give us both time to think. "Sensible!" I was being pulled in two directions, which was a new experience and I didn't like it.

As soon as John greeted me, he told me there was a letter. I took it from its prominent place on the mantleshelf and made to dash upstairs, noting the knowing looks.

"Go on," John said, "take your letter and get yourself washed while I take your things upstairs. Ellen will get us a cup of tea." He bent down and lifted my bag from the floor. "Go on," he urged, "I can see you're dying to read it!"

I knew they would not press me, but I would tell them. They would understand.

"Take your time. Your tea will be waiting."

Alone, I sat on the bed and tore the letter open. As I read I could hear his voice. It was as if he was in the room.

My Dear Doris,

While you are away, please look back to what has been happening to us. Do not think of the time we have known one another, but at the marvellous unfolding of something tremendous for us. Ponder on how nearly we missed meeting, a matter of seconds, and you would have left the dance hall. My first letter to you — the chance of you getting it was very small — yet it found you!

Doris, it's inevitable that we should be together. Don't try to play "safe". Accept events. What I feel for you is an indescribable desire to share your life. Please understand that this is not a game. Our meeting reminds me of your words from a Greek philosopher — two halves of a circle wandering about until they form a circle of kindred souls. No other girl could do this for me. I shall think of you constantly and long for your return.

Tom

Tom's letter brought my emotions sharply into focus. He had seen the opportunity for us to spend time together. Now I realised that almost casually I had rejected that offer. More than ever at that moment I wanted desperately to be with Tom. I wrote immediately to tell him that my visit to London was to be shortened. My brother was talking about the seriousness of international events, the likelihood of war. A further incentive was not required but it did confirm my resolve even more firmly.

The meeting with Tom was emotional. He had a flood of questions. His main concern was that his letter had been too outspoken for me, but he need not have worried. He was clearly fearing that I may have returned to end our relationship.

I explained in the best way that I could that his letter had had such an impact on my emotions that I felt compelled to return early.

It was a beautiful spring evening. Our immediate world was full of beauty and peace.

We discussed world events. My brother had told me that Mussolini and Hitler were marching their armies into other countries and just taking over. Poland seemed next on Hitler's list. The cold shock of horror had really struck home when he had said that this war, for he was certain it would happen, would not be fought on land, in trenches, but in the air. Those words "in the air" filled me with such deep foreboding I could hardly bear it.

That evening I knew that there was a bond between Tom and me. I also knew that nothing would ever completely break it.

CHAPTER
FOUR

After Easter

We met the following Saturday evening. I had promised to show Tom one of my favourite woods, near the oak tree.

Its floor was covered by oxlips at that time of year. Tom was intrigued as I explained that they look like a cross between a cowslip and a primrose. They made a breathtaking scene, complete with an unforgettable perfume. It was an evocative sweet smell.

I remember the stillness of that scene and can still conjure up the feeling of sanctuary provided by the trees that enclosed us in apparent security.

Here we first kissed and knew that we were meant for each other. Tom expressed a great urgency. He saw beyond the consummation of our love. He told me that he wanted to share my love of books and the theatre, to know me more, to know my family, to marry me!

There was also a deep sadness. He told me that he believed that time would be short. He meant this but I could not really understand.

We picked wild flowers that day. We knew they would not survive long after being plucked out of their natural surroundings.

That evening we walked towards Haverhill, hand in hand in quiet contemplation.

At our next meeting I had decided to show Tom a different view of the town. We took a bridle path edged by tall trees. I wanted to show Tom something of great meaning to me. It was a square stone memorial set into the ground, now overgrown. I parted the grass so that Tom could read the inscription.

Near this place lie the remains of Poker for many years the favourite mare of Josiah Boreham and later W. Boreham.
She never made a false step.

I told him how as a child I had come to put wild flowers on this grave. In my imagination she had been a gallant charger with a brave knight on her back. That day I was able to share something from my childhood with Tom. He was more than worthy. It was also the day that I gave him a copy of Omar Khayyam's poetry, which I loved. I hoped that he would learn to love the work as much as I did. He took the book, which became a treasure to him.

24

The walk led to ground higher than the town. Church, chapel and factory were clear below us. Tom was obviously surprised as I explained the presence of a family weaving firm which gave employment to many. He had thought of the area as exclusively rural, with farming the only big enterprise. Compared with his north-east home, that would be a true picture. I told him how some workers had been laid off. Clearly this struck a deep chord with Tom. He tried to explain that the south had been spared from the effects of the Depression. He was right.

"Where I come from," he told me, "no man in my street had a job. There was no hope of one either. Men and women have been destroyed by poverty." Then with bitter irony in his voice he remarked that things were better now in the shipyards because they were building ships for the war.

I felt the innocence of a protected childhood. My life had been sheltered, steady and predictable. But now I understood how the lack of jobs and poverty must have forced men like Tom into the services. Sensitive, peace-loving men who only wanted the chance to lead quiet lives, marry, have children and grow old in time. In other words, Tom had no great ambition except to follow the natural order of life. As for countless others, it was not to be.

"The only wonderful thing about joining the RAF and being sent to Number Nine Squadron at Stradishall is meeting you, Doris," Tom explained. I knew that he meant every word.

I could see that to grow I needed to expand my horizons. Tom had also helped me to understand that the world existed elsewhere and perhaps I should be courageous enough to explore.

But I too had my experience of books to offer. I gave him my copy of *The Rubáiyat of Omar Khayyám* to read. Tom had already told my how he loved *Hiawatha*. We began to open up new worlds for each other.

CHAPTER
FIVE

Apart

We met each Saturday evening, falling easily into a comfortable routine, so much so that it was hard to remember life without Tom. I was more relaxed, sure of my feelings. I felt that our relationship was meant to be. I accepted "us" as a couple and tried not contemplate the future. Each moment was precious and, looking back, I realise my desire to preserve them all.

So, when we met as usual on a Saturday evening in May, my heart sank as Tom desolately broke the news that he was soon to be sent away until the end of July. It was a navigation course at Hamble Water near Southampton. I experienced the numbing pain of loss. I could sense his bitter disappointment. Tom had tried to be positive, suggesting that we could meet in London. I could stay with my brother.

I was defeated, wanted to end our relationship there and then. But Tom's strength and determination was greater than mine at this point.

He again declared his love with greater passion than ever, compared himself to a young salmon, fighting, struggling to swim upstream against the tide, because it knew through a force far greater than itself that it must continue, whatever the cost.

He told me again how he wanted us to marry, be together and share everything.

I was won again by this love, his sincerity.

The next Saturday Tom was able to tell me how he had been allowed a short visit home during the week. He wanted to see his beloved mother before the enforced absence, and to tell her about me. Tom returned to Suffolk early, impatient to see me. He told me how some of his fellow airmen had noticed his distraction and lack of interest in drinking, and that he spent his free time reading. A certain amount of teasing had taken place. Tom largely brushed it off. He told me that they just did not understand how he felt.

That evening we discussed Omar Khayyám. We decided our favourite verse was

Ah Love! Could thou and I with Fate conspire
To grasp this sorry Scheme of Things entire,

"It's our verse," Tom said softly.

We were nostalgic already for those peaceful country evenings. I knew that I had to commit this to memory. The air was bursting with birdsong, cows munched serenely in the meadows, and sheep's parsley perfumed a perfect scene.

Tom told me something of his family that evening. He was extremely close to his mother. He had felt her loneliness more keenly than ever during his leave. He explained that his father had been gassed during the First World War. He was now unable to work well. The whole experience had left him a bitter and broken man. Tom's mother loved him so much and must have had such fears for her son that for her to become enthusiastic about a young woman, a complete stranger, was too much to expect. Tom had told his mother about me, about his plans, but she had not been curious. Not yet, anyway.

Tom had been braver than I was. My family knew nothing about him. I had not known where to start in telling them. Life was safer that way.

I had been thrown back to the earlier feelings of uncertainty about our relationship. Tom never once wavered in his belief in us as a couple. He displayed incredible patience with me. It must have been the strength of his certainty that kept us together. He tried to be strong for both of us, but never took liberties with my affection. He was always perfectly behaved.

That evening our parting had a different feel. Tom gave me his new address at Hamble. He wanted me to write and arrange our meetings in London to coincide with times when I could visit my brother there. He seemed so positive that this would be a solution. Tom even joked that we could meet as often as before.

That evening I kissed him without inhibition and very publicly. I too had a strong conviction about us and was beginning to be able to express my emotion. I did not care who saw us. An imminent parting can really focus the mind.

CHAPTER
SIX

London

During the next week I received a short letter from Tom arranging for us to meet the following Saturday at 7 p.m. under the clock at Charing Cross station. It seems that time watched over us in many ways, marking significant events, allowing us to meet and yet always casting an ominous shadow, marking our partings, racing on when we wished its passing to be slow, slowing to sometimes, an unbearable pace when we waited to meet again.

Certainly, clocks are highly suitable landmarks as meeting places. But time the tormentor is there always and no one can ignore it. Perhaps meeting under clocks is a silent plea from lovers for special dispensation, a kind of credit for the rightness of our feelings; a hope that time will see us and slow down as a reward because we are special. I know this is dreaming, and we shall always dream.

We both suffered anxiety before that meeting. So it was with a mixture of pure joy and relief that we met that evening. We stood gazing at each other, making sure that this was really true. An onlooker might have thought we had been apart for years and were noting how we had changed.

It had taken a certain degree of courage for me to travel to London to meet Tom. I know now this was the first step in thinking for myself, leading my own life. Tom's experiences in the RAF and living away from home meant that he truly had become much more grown-up and worldly than me. My life had seemed so predictable before Tom. Somehow, although it was not actually said, there seemed an acceptance that I would remain a teacher and live at home for many years to come. Of course then marriage was out of the question because women teachers were not allowed to marry, and had to leave the profession if they did. As no one had come even remotely close to this suggestion I somehow imagined that my life was set in a pattern that would continue. Now I realise that was a simplistic view of life. But then I did feel I had been locked into a pattern. Tom had already shown me that life could be different, deliciously unpredictable and challenging.

We found a Lyons Corner House. A great institution now long gone. The great feature of a Lyons was you could guarantee a reasonable cup of tea, a warm place to sit and talk, and peace if not quiet. No one hassled you to move on, and one cup of tea and a cake could last. Tom loved the normality of this situation. He found RAF life difficult in many ways. How he missed the tinkling of a spoon on a teacup, the homely things of life. Whilst in London he stayed at the Union Jack Club. Bed and breakfast cost £1 for the night.

Tom wanted to talk about my family — he was eager to meet them. I knew that I was loved and trusted, but I was not yet ready to allow my family to share Tom. He quickly understood that I preferred to talk about other things. After all, I had come to London; no one had prevented me, so he assumed that all was well.

He told me about his new life at Hamble. The early weeks were theory instructions and he was enjoying the challenge and relishing the experience. He admitted that it was hard work, so intense that he was spending evenings in study. Tom wanted to do well, and looked forward to the practical application of his new navigational skills as a kind of reward. I think he felt it was a distraction from loneliness and also something positive to hold on to. At least as a navigator he would not have to fly in the rear of the plane, a gunner and vulnerable. This thought gave him a crumb of comfort.

I tried to encourage him to forget, not think bleakly of the future. He became very serious and I realised the naivety of this remark. He told me that it was always there in the background, the beating of a drum; it never ceased. He had accepted it before we met. Now he wished with all his heart that it would go away. He became wistful, quoting our verse again, "Ah love, if thou and I with Fate conspire to grasp this sorry Scheme of things entire." I listened intently, gazing into his eyes. He leaned across, lightly touching my cheek, stroking my hair. We were the only two people in the world.

He broke the spell, reminding me that we had all tomorrow to be together. The prospect was enchanting.

We decided to take a bus to Piccadilly Circus. I was immediately reminded of New Year's Eve. You may remember that my family had been together with my brother at Parsons Green. That evening, the last of 1938, I had gone to the theatre to see *Geneva* by Bernard Shaw. It was a play for our time, with the characters of Hitler, Franco and Mussolini strutting about the stage extolling their might. I felt a cold shiver as I spoke, explaining to Tom that events seemed so linked. I had seen the play, Hitler had "walked" into Austria. I felt it impossible to believe, sitting in that normal atmosphere in London, that Hitler had also walked into Czechoslovakia just about the time Tom and I had met.

That night, after the theatre, I found myself caught up in crowds of New Year revellers. There was singing and a real party mood in the streets. But that year there was something else. We had experienced the Munich crisis, there were rumours of war and the Prime Minister was being criticised for his handling of the situation. I did not fully understand, but that night there were chants of "Chamberlain must go" mixed in with "Auld Lang Syne", and the muffled chimes of Big Ben striking midnight were all but drowned out by the noise from the crowds. I had not expected so many people. The underground had closed, but I just managed to catch the last bus towards home. It stopped a long way short, leaving me to walk the rest. Eventually I arrived at 4 a.m. really worried that my brother would have reported me missing. Of course all was well and I can laugh now.

The next day, Sunday, remains for me one of those perfect experiences. We met in the morning under "our" clock, both with a confidence and joy we were eager to embrace. It was a beautiful early summer's day. We kissed with great emotion, we knew this was right, we were meant for each other.

We walked in Kew Gardens, talking, laughing, watching, completely absorbed by each other. I felt moments "as big as years". That day is still so vivid, but there is no memory of eating or drinking, the ordinary stuff of life. It was our day, producing a happiness that sustained us both when we parted, slipping back into our respective responsibilities much stronger and able to endure the week ahead because we had become one.

We settled into what was almost a routine, for we met in London on alternate weekends. In between we wrote long precious letters.

One weekend I suggested that we went to see Shaw's *Geneva* at the Westminster Theatre. I had enjoyed the play so much and wanted to introduce Tom to the theatre. It was a new and important event for him. He was absorbed and moved by the whole experience. He sat with his eyes closed after the final curtain. To Tom it was a revelation. He told me how reading, discussing books and now the theatre were opening his mind, for which he had me to thank. I shared the memory of my first experience of the theatre with Tom. It was at the Arts Theatre in Cambridge. The play was J.B. Priestley's *Time and the Conways*. I had been spellbound, completely involved in the drama on stage. At the end I had felt the final curtain was an intrusion. So I understood the impact that live theatre must have had on Tom. We had discovered yet another love. That theatre visit with Tom was an unforgettable evening.

Tom's only previous visit to a live performance had been when quite young. At 13 he had been on a coach trip to the Albert Hall to see a performance of *Hiawatha*. Even at such a young age he had felt moved to tears by Hiawatha's wooing of Minnehaha. Hiawatha as a character remained an inspiration to Tom. He carried a pocket edition with him at all times. I have it still today.

CHAPTER
SEVEN

Long Leave

About halfway through his course Tom was given a long leave and, very significantly, a railway warrant. He decided to stay at the Bell Hotel in Haverhill.

Tom was eager to meet my family. It was his decision to spend his leave in this way. He wrote to tell me. Excitement was mixed with anxiety. I was unsure of what to say to my parents so I left everything to Tom.

Tom called at the house for me. You must remember that even though I was working I did not enjoy the freedom and apparent self-confidence of today's young people. My parents had strong views about how I should live my life and at that time they did not include a stranger to the town and certainly not an airman. I saw later that their lack of enthusiasm at meeting Tom was completely coloured by their role as my protectors. They were benevolent dictators. They wanted what was best for me and always did their best. There was of course that much-debated generation gap between us, fuelled by fear, lack of understanding and probably a degree of prejudice. They could not stop me seeing Tom. That first evening when he "called" for me, Tom was so understanding. He suggested a day in Cambridge, where we could talk and be ourselves. He was always so positive, such was the strength of his belief in us!

That evening we had to walk home through lightning. I was afraid. Tom gently shaded my eyes with his handkerchief and led me to safety. He was so sensitive to others' feelings, too humane to be a willing aggressor.

The following day Tom called for me in time to catch the 10 a.m. train to Cambridge. I was nervous, uneasy about my family's cool reaction to Tom and did not know what to say to him. I rattled off a suggested itinerary, "Visit King's College, watch punts on the River Cam, eat at Lyons," etc.

Tom just looked at me and I remember just as the train pulled into the platform he kissed me. I knew his sincerity and deep love at that moment. We hoped, as any young couple heady with love, that we would have the carriage to ourselves. But we were joined by a woman rather flustered by her situation. She was charged with taking her three-year-old grandson to hospital in Cambridge. Apparently he had managed to lodge a grain of wheat in his ear. Tom was sympathetic. Like the perfect gentleman, he helped them into a taxi from the station and wished them good luck.

We began our day of taking in the sights. I told Tom about Rupert Brooke and his famous poem, "Grantchester". Time again in our thoughts.

> Stands the church clock at ten to three?
> And is there honey still for tea?

Tom listened, enthralled, as I became more animated, more enthusiastic about Rupert Brooke, who as you probably know died far too young, at the time of the First World War.

I quoted my real favourite;

> Is it the hour? We leave this resting place
> Made fair by one another for a while . . .
> Do you think there is a far border town
>   somewhere
> The desert's edge, last of the lands we know . . .
> In which I'll find you waiting; and we'll go
> Together, hand in hand again out there . . .*

* *The Wayfarers*, by Rupert Brooke.

I could not recall the whole poem but wanted Tom to understand the sense of it, suggesting this verse fitted us. What we needed was more time. Perhaps I was beginning to hear the drumbeats in Tom's head.

We ambled along the cobbled streets that day, strolled through the ancient colleges, finding ourselves at lunchtime near the Senate House, back into the real world in search of a Lyons. Tom admitted that funds were short. He was spending the little money he had on travel to London to meet me. I really did not mind and had not expected a banquet. We found Lyons and managed to afford fish and chips with a pot of tea.

This day was so pleasant I did not want it to end. Tom was more direct. We tackled the difficult question of my feeling torn between Tom and family. The one thing I seemed unable to do at that stage was to see us as a couple, strong together.

I found myself expressing the view, not without discomfort, that this was something that I would have to solve alone. Also I was unhappy, not ready to make choices if I had to, between all the people that I loved.

Unable to resolve this complex range of emotions, we became silent. Tom must have felt that our relationship was at a standstill. We parted coolly that evening. We both felt we had lost each other.

CHAPTER
EIGHT

Realisation

During the next few weeks I threw myself into work believing that would solve all problems. Of course it did not. At weekends and in the evenings there was time to think. I began to brood.

One weekend I took the train to Long Melford, and set off to walk to the beautiful village of Lavenham. I particularly admired the splendid church built by wealthy merchants. Standing gazing up at the familiar tower and high roof, my thoughts turned to Tom. I imagined him in a plane soaring like an eagle into the open sky. I knew I missed him and now had lost hope. He had been absolutely right in his wish for us to be strong together and I had not seen his strength.

Just when I thought all hope had gone I received a letter.

Hamble.
July, 1939

Doris

I have found it most difficult to concentrate on my work these last few weeks. Thank goodness it will soon be finished and I shall have some leave. These few lines from Hiawatha say all that I feel, Doris.

As unto the bow the cord is
So unto the man is woman
Though she bends him she obeys him
Though she draws him, yet she follows
Useless each without the other.
Thus the youthful Hiawatha
Said within himself and pondered
Much perplexed by various feelings
Listless, longing, hoping, fearing
Dreaming still of Minnehaha.

Even the strongest at times feel unequal to their task in life, especially when they know love as I know it, and as our dusky friend above knew it. Please write to me, Doris. I shall be going home at the end of the course. Surely you are due to break up at the end of July? Whatever happens,

I must come to see you before I go North. We are at a standstill while world events are running ahead rapidly.

Tom.

I sank down into a chair and closing my eyes, mulled over every word to be reassured that Tom still loved and wanted me. I smiled, opened my eyes again and went to school that morning with a light heart, chafing against the slowness of the hours. When the last lesson was over I literally ran home and, refusing a cup of tea, dashed upstairs to find my copy of *Hiawatha*. Slowly I read the extract, which opened the chapter "Hiawatha's Wooing". I read it several times then settled down to write to Tom.

Haverhill.
July, 1939.

Tom,
Oh thank you for writing and for the extract. I have just re-read it and Tom, my heart does so want to speak. I break up at the end of the week. I shall not go away until I have seen you, and, like Minnehaha, I shall be thinking — only I shall be thinking of an airman from another

town and county, young and not too tall and very handsome! Please call for me!

Doris.

P. S. I hope I haven't wasted too much time.

The last few days of term ran their course too slowly for me but finally, three days later, a telegram arrived early in the morning:

Calling for you tomorrow evening, Tom.

I could not believe it — Tom coming tomorrow — and then I realised "tomorrow" in fact meant "today". The telegram had been sent yesterday. "It will be today! Soon I shall be with him!" my heart sang. The expression on my face, reflected in the bedroom mirror, was one of complete happiness.

"Doris," my mother's voice called up the stairs, dragging me back to reality. "Doris, can you get some vegetables for me please?"

"Just coming," I called back.

I was suddenly anxious to tell someone, to share my happiness. I decided to call on my friend Phyllis Harrap and confide in her my rediscovered joy.

My very dear friends Walter and Phyllis Harrap lived in a comfortable house on the outskirts of the town. I had met Walter through the dramatic society. They were an amazing couple, who had often welcomed me and my good friend Marion into their home for wonderful evenings of laughter and conversation. They were people to whom I could talk easily and be myself with. They were kind and understanding. They had introduced me to the plays of J.B. Priestley. Walter worked in a bank, his wife was an artist. Somehow we could talk about any subject with them. An important part of the friendship was that they did not make judgements and accepted people as themselves, without expectations. In their house and company I relaxed and blossomed.

I had told Phyllis about Tom. Our lives were busy, so it was mainly in the holidays that I could visit Phyllis. Imagine the excitement and anticipation that afternoon when I called to tell them that Tom would be calling for me that evening. Phyllis had made me most welcome. We sat drinking lemonade and I told the story of how Tom and I had met. It must have been obvious how much Tom meant to me. Phyllis was caught up in my mood. It was a relief to tell her of my feelings. After listening intently for some time, Phyllis made a suggestion. She had taken her only son to stay with his cousins that morning. Walter and Phyllis planned to walk over to visit her mother that evening and so the house would be empty. And so it was that she gave me a key, inviting me to take Tom to the house so that we could spend time together alone.

I felt so many emotions joy, excitement, anticipation at seeing Tom again, when all had seemed hopeless, also deep gratitude towards my friend for both her understanding and the trust she placed in me and Tom, who was as yet a complete stranger to her. I readily accepted.

I prepared for Tom's visit with feverish excitement. When the knock came, I flew to the door and we fell into each other's arms, kissing, hugging and laughing all at once. There was a new confidence within me which Tom responded to immediately when I told him of the plans to be alone at my friends' house.

We re-established ourselves as a couple very quickly. I hardly recall the details of walking to the Harraps'. Just a hazy memory of happiness. That evening was to be more memorable than I could have imagined. Tom wanted everything to be perfect. He asked me to go with him to Northumberland for a holiday to meet his parents. He enthused about the places he would show me, the castles of Alnwick and Bamburgh, the hills . . . Then he told me that if his parents were unwilling, which he doubted, he would return immediately to me and make other arrangements. He laughed about the prospect of staying in Youth Hostels in the Cheviot Hills. With him as navigator, how could we get lost? And then, quite sure that I knew I loved him, he asked me to marry him. My answer was given instantly. "Yes, yes! I want to marry you, Tom."

More strongly than ever, we burned with desire to consummate our love. But time and place were against us. Also Tom showed such control, along with his deep determination to behave correctly, especially as we were guests in a friend's house. A great deal had happened to us in a short time. Very soon the Harraps returned and I very proudly introduced Tom to them. We talked easily, telling them our news. They could sense our happiness and were caught up in the joy, sealing it with their sincere good wishes for our future together.

I lacked the confidence to tell my parents of our plans that evening, but agreed to follow Tom to Northumberland as soon as he had seen and spoken to his parents.

Tom stayed at the Bell Hotel that night. I was to travel to Cambridge with him the next day to see him off on his journey home. He had told me how he had been unable to sleep. He was so impatient now for us to marry that he had wished in some ways that we had not waited. Deep down, Tom knew that would hurt his mother, something he could not bear.

Tom called at the house the next morning. He confidently asked my parents if he could take me to visit his parents. Of course I was free to do as I wished with my holiday, but politeness was one of Tom's outstanding qualities.

Tom wanted me to go with him there and then. He resolved to send me a telegram as soon as possible confirming my visit.

It was a difficult parting. They always were. As the Newcastle train left the platform Tom repeated "Until tomorrow" and lastly "Tomorrow our Tomorrow." These words stayed with me all the way back from Cambridge. The wheels turning on the track seemed to mock me "tomorrow, tomorrow, tomorrow."

I recalled the words from Omar Khayyám.

Tomorrow? Why, tomorrow I may be
Myself with Yesterday's Seven thousand Years.

I felt so alone in that railway carriage. Tom had truly won my heart. I could never be the same again. He would always be there, whatever happened for the rest of my life.

Tom told me later how his parents agreed to meeting the girl he was to marry. He was pleasantly surprised not so much by his mother's reaction but by his father's. They were not close. But on this visit they had common ground. Tom's father, so badly disabled in the First World War, could see the signs of the next one all too clearly. They both agreed that war was likely. There was not much to say but they had understood each other. Tom felt for his father's loss and suffering. He understood his bitterness a little more. Tom's father forgot his own feelings and thought of his dear son and the danger that war would bring to him, to them all. He despaired of mankind.

The blow fell more quickly than anticipated. It was July, a glorious summer. Tom had been at home for a few short hours when a telegram arrived for him.

Leave cancelled, return to your squadron immediately

was the terrible message.

Tom and his father both knew that the war was now almost inevitable.

Tom felt at that point that he would never walk with me in those beloved hills. It was the beginning of the end. He went back to his room, where just a few hours ago he had flung down his rucksack with a light heart. All that happiness had drained away.

Meanwhile I prepared for our holiday. My parents had expected that I might spend time with my friend Hilary. They still had not fully accepted the proposal for me to visit Northumberland with Tom, even though he had been to the house and explained the plans. For me this was a big step into the new way of life. I was so glad to be facing a new adventure away from routine. More importantly, the prospect of spending time with Tom was simply wonderful.

I packed, leaving my cases in the hall. I remember drinking tea that morning, studying the family photographs in the sitting room. Those images, meant a great deal but just then I sensed a feeling of being suffocated by a family that wanted me to remain close. I experienced the urge to get away, be myself and discover new horizons.

No doubt, today's young people feel similar emotions. It is natural, I know that now. The lucky ones leave for college or university, but the opportunities had not been available to me. It took another lever to prise me from the parental grasp.

I was apprehensive but prepared for the adventure. It was with great sadness and shock that I received Tom's telegram.

Darling, don't come. Recalled to squadron. Leave cancelled.

Love Tom.

Everything fell apart. It was a savage blow. I fled to my room and wept tears of deep pain. What should have been a happy time had in a moment disintegrated into a nightmare. I feared for Tom. The recall must mean war. The prospect was too terrible to contemplate.

During those next dark days Phyllis Harrap listened, soothed my fears, tried to reassure me — in fact was everything that a dear friend can be. Without her support I could not have borne that time until, as she said it would, a letter finally arrived from Tom.

Somewhere in England
August

My dearest Doris,

It seems a lifetime since I last saw you. When I got that telegram, I ached with sadness for things not to be. And what of you, Doris, not knowing my whereabouts? I felt so helpless. You said you would marry me when I next see you. I hope you will agree to my making arrangements for the wedding.

I cannot begin to tell you what the thought of this does to me.

Out of all this chaos and uncertainty, you and I are constant. Like a beacon light, you, Doris, are shining through the darkness of the present.

I remember you standing on Cambridge station, wearing that blue flowered frock. So slim and beautiful you looked. I wanted to lose myself in your eyes, gazing at me with love and trust.

"Till tomorrow," I said. I should have taken you with me, then we should at least had one "day", and perhaps you would have enjoyed staying with my parents. They were looking forward to meeting you. My father surprised me. He had lost some of his remoteness, and I felt I could be close to him eventually.

To come back to you, my dearest. I've wanted you from the moment I first saw you. You intrigue me, and you are a constant delight to me: the way you walk, the way you look at me when you are listening to me. Your face is so expressive, Doris — I come alive when I'm with you.

My mind will be constantly with you until I see you again. Until then, my dearest, take care of yourself and hold onto "us".

Tom

I read it twice, with mixed feelings of relief and the need for his physical presence. "This is one of the great moments, Tom. Yes, I will marry you! I want to belong to you." I recalled the Sunday morning we spent trying to discover the skylark's nest — watching the bird high up, listening to it sing its heart out, following its descent to earth, running to the spot — no nest! How we had laughed and rolled over and over in the grass with the sheer joy of it all. But that had been all. I wondered if Tom had wanted to kiss me then. One day I would ask him.

A few days later Russia and Germany made a non-aggression pact. The talk was only of war. It was, as has often been said, a beautiful hot summer. All this talk of aggression and invasion seemed unreal. Those who had seen war before were more pessimistic. On 1 September Germany invaded Poland. We were heading for the inevitable.

Everyone who was there remembers Sunday 3 September, 1939. The summer holidays were at an end. All around the country schools were restarting. In our house, Sunday teatime, that great tradition went ahead, a kind of defiance of world events. I did enjoy the certainty of this ritual. But that Sunday there was tension, uneasy silence and underlying fear.

My father, ever practical, suggested that we took a walk. We walked to "our" oak tree. I was in a dream with Tom and probably poor company for my father, who loved to talk.

We met a man, a well-known local character. He was gassed in the First World War. His opinions were strong and doom-laden.

"Make no mistake about it, he's got it all. He can wipe us out. It wouldn't surprise me if he came tonight and gassed the lot of us. It wouldn't surprise me at all." He spoke as if he knew Hitler personally and was privy to his thoughts and plans. If it had not been so terrible a prediction it would have been funny.

But underlying his warning was the acknowledgement that we were no match for an invader. Certainly, Tom had hinted that our air force was undermanned, undertrained and using inadequate aircraft. There were many problems with the Wellington bombers. The crews had little protection if they were hit. There was a great danger of fire. At the time the public knew very little about these realities, and as the war progressed our aircraft improved greatly.

CHAPTER
NINE

The War Begins

Tom told me later something of his feelings about the day war was declared. The atmosphere at the air base was tense, so the news when it came brought an element of relief. The waiting was over. Everything they did from then on was for real, but his thoughts were with me. He had no stomach for war and had been caught up in events over which he had no control, though they concerned his life directly. It was no ordinary job where you could make decisions about leaving if it was not to your taste. The country was at war. Tom, along with the best of the nation's young men, was required to serve. There was no way out.

He had reflected on how much Suffolk now meant to him because of us. It was ironic that he was at his most happy whilst being in mortal danger at the same time.

There were surprises in store for Tom. The following day they were to fly over the Kiel Canal German naval base. They had expected only to fly at night, as their training and motto indicated. After that daytime mission Tom realised just how vulnerable the planes were, easy targets in the light. Tom admitted his fear to me but duty came above everything else.

His life became increasingly tough. Leave was almost impossible to obtain. It was extremely difficult to communicate with friends or family outside the air base. The base accommodation was so stretched that soon they were living in tents. The base was on standby, meaning that they were called on for briefing at any time. It could be an exercise or a real mission. He soon experienced being under fire from the German anti-aircraft fire. It was frightening, to say the least.

This time until the end of 1939 was known as the "phoney war". Many people thought the conflict would be "all over" by Christmas. That was not the case and our best young men were in the line of fire.

Tom knew that the radio kept the public informed of events. It was difficult for me. I wanted to listen but became more fearful of what I might hear.

There began to be reports of air raids from which planes had not returned. Men were reported missing. We heard how sometimes they were picked up from the freezing water of the North

Sea. My heart was chilled by that phrase, "reported missing".

In those first days of conflict I held on to my faith and belief in Tom. My work enabled me to maintain some sense of reality, but deep down my anxiety grew.

It was a beautiful autumn. That we were at war seemed unbelievable at times.

Weeks passed. October arrived. There was still no word from Tom. My sense of isolation increased. I knew no one else in the same situation and it was hard to talk about Tom at home. My father had even tried to suggest that I should forget him as we might never meet again. Phyllis was a great comfort; without her I could not have borne that time of darkness.

One evening, I had been marking books, my mind not fully on the task, when there was a knock on the door, which jolted me back to reality.

It was Tom. I stared in disbelief for an instant. A torrent of emotion surged through us both. We clung to each other for support.

When we had recovered some composure, I suggested a walk. It was just getting dark, there was a beautiful moon. I was aware of the echo from our footsteps. They seemed to reinforce the underlying sadness of our situation.

Tom told me something of his experiences, but mostly of his feelings. He was bitter that we had been deprived of our holiday. He felt frustration at our enforced separation, the misery of his daily life and the growing realisation that our lives were governed by forces beyond our control. He felt as if caught in a net. He was not free.

It is very hard for those who did not live through those times to understand how difficult it was for us young people. We had our lives ahead of us but absolutely no power over the direction they would take. That was an element of the "freedom" fought and died for. Of course it was more complex than that. The instinct to defend home territory from invasion is incredibly strong in mankind. Tom suffered from thinking too deeply about his situation. He had such sensitivity for life, and could see history repeating itself. Man had learned little from the slaughter of the First World War.

But it was conflict that had brought us together. We had to learn to live with that. The uncertainty, the tearful partings and emotional reunions all seemed to heighten the feelings of the time. There must have been countless wartime relationships like ours. Perhaps we could not have survived those terrible times without believing in someone, and wishing for a better future.

Fear of invasion from Germany was a strong and real emotion. We had heard how Poland had been invaded extremely quickly. Many people felt that we were vulnerable and that we would also be invaded. People in Tom's position knew in more detail about the strength of the German war machine and how in the early stages of the war we could not match it. Our aeroplanes, for instance, were initially easy targets for the Germans, whose RADAR equipment and techniques were superior. That changed later. But for those airmen who were the first to engage in conflict, their task was difficult and dangerous. They did not flinch from their duty.

Tom had a brief leave. He stayed at the Bell Hotel again, meeting me from school. By that time I was working just outside the town. I cycled to work. For those few days Tom met me in the afternoon. We walked towards home, Tom pushing the bike for me. It was a strange time, as if life was a film and the frames were frozen for a brief respite before it rolled to an inevitable end.

We could not believe the contrast between that spectacularly golden autumn and the appalling conflict in Europe.

Tom was not supposed to tell me about his missions, and I do not suppose it matters now, except that he must have felt so horrified he had to speak to someone. He told me not to repeat his stories. Of course at the time and for many years afterwards I did not say a word.

The aspect that caused Tom most distress was that after all the training and the motto about night flying, they were now flying in daylight. He knew that made them sitting targets. The absurdity of his situation dominated his thoughts.

Wrapped in this intense mood, Tom proposed to me. We planned to marry as soon as was practical. There would be little time to organise and make arrangements, but our union was inevitable.

The following evening we visited our friends the Harraps. They were delighted as well as understanding of our situation. This was hardly a traditional engagement. But we were living in exceptional times.

We discussed telling my parents. That evening Tom bravely and formally asked my father for his permission to marry me. Of course, legally it was unnecessary. It was, though, a reassuringly normal thing to do amidst the uncertainty of those times.

My father, a wise man, indicated to Tom that he considered it a hasty step. He only cared about my happiness, and now I understand his concern. Tom did not hold back in declaring his love for me. He told my parents how his only desire was to love, protect and cherish me always.

They were unable to approve, but also did not seek to stop us.

As Tom left the house that evening, we agreed to marry on his next leave, even though neither of us could predict the timing. I planned to give up my job. As a married man Tom could live off base.

The next day I awoke to find a letter from Tom. He must have posted it through the letterbox very early on his way back to the base. My father had left it on the breakfast table.

I read eagerly.

My Dear Wife-to-be,

You will be asleep when I put this through the letter box. I couldn't sleep, so I got up early and, as my mind was full of you, I just had to write to you. I do hope you won't have too much friction with your parents over our marriage. The Harraps were right — I'm glad I told them. I shall write to my parents as soon as I finish this, to tell them the wonderful news. I hope they will be happy about it. I truly regret that we can't have a traditional wedding.

Don't think I'm unaware of the seriousness of the step we're taking. Forget that I've only known you since March. Since then I've come alive in every possible way, for you bring out qualities in me I didn't know I possessed.

I accept that we were meant for each other. The circle is complete. I now wait with impatience and frustration for the time when you will come to me. Will you remember this, my dear Doris?

Tom

That letter sustained me for many weeks. I was to hear nothing more from Tom until November.

CHAPTER
TEN

Mr and Mrs Tom English

The fifth of November will never be forgotten by me for reasons other than Guy Fawkes and the Gunpowder Plot.

It was my parents' wedding anniversary and in 1939 they had arranged to travel to London to spend the day with my brother John. They must have felt the need to see him and no doubt were concerned about how the war might affect his life. It was a Saturday, my father would be free from work. Indeed, I might even have gone with them. But it was not to be.

During the previous evening Tom's long-awaited telegram had arrived. I knew what it would say, hardly needing to open it. We were having our evening meal. The room was hot from a blazing fire, but I felt the atmosphere to have been chilled by the shock that my parents felt. I can still recall the rush of mixed emotions on receiving that red telegram. I was afraid to read it but at the same time knew that this was the news that was to change my life for ever. Sometimes we make decisions from which there is no turning back ever; we follow a path knowing that the way ahead will be difficult, but if driven by conviction, or in this case overwhelming love, there is really no choice. My will seemed suspended at that point even though somewhere deep down I recognised that I had gladly made the decision to marry Tom. That decision had caused heartache. My parents were fearful of my actions, wanting only the best, which should have included a church wedding in Haverhill, in true family tradition, to some respectable local young man with a sure future. It should, in their eyes, have been the joining of known families. I would then take my place in continuing the life of this quiet and settled community.

But it was not just in my life that change was so significant. Everything was changing in response to the war, and the hardships had hardly begun.

So it was with a mixture of fear and excitement that I opened Tom's telegram on the evening of 4 November 1939.

It was short and to the point.

All arrangements made. Stop. Come Tomorrow. Stop. Saturday to Bury St Edmunds. Stop. Wedding at 11am. Stop. Love Tom.

That evening I re-read Tom's last letter to me. I could hardly believe how much he loved me. The last few months replayed in my mind. Each time Tom was there, sure and consistent in his belief in us. It had been there from the moment we met. He had enough strength for us both, which was needed more than ever now.

I slept well that night, probably too exhausted by events to allow excitement to keep me awake.

Just before 7 a.m. on Saturday 5 November 1939 I was drinking tea brought by my father and preparing for the most significant day in my life so far.

My father came with me to the station. I had packed a small case but did not know exactly what Tom had planned. As the train puffed into the station, my father asked me gravely if I knew what I was doing. We had stood like stuffed dummies until that point. I had really no reply to console him, just my belief in Tom. Sending my love to John and Ellen via my parents, I left Haverhill for the journey to Bury St Edmunds.

I remember few details of that journey except that it was dark and extremely long. Today the town seems so near, a short car journey on a good road or even a reasonably pleasant bus ride on market day, through familiar countryside. That day all lights were blacked out because of the war.

The train was slow, not direct. Luckily I was alone in the carriage. Somehow this felt peaceful. Not having to make polite conversation with other passengers came as a great relief. All my energies had gone into reaching this point. I needed time and peace to gather myself together. I had dressed smartly but hardly looked the part of a bride. There was no hat.

As the journey progressed, I began to feel more light-hearted. A wave of optimism replaced some of my fears. "Home" felt much further away that it was and my desire to be in Tom's arms increased with each rhythmic rumble along the track. It was strange then, that as the train stopped at Bury St Edmunds station, a wave of panic swept over me. I sat unable to move. A matter of seconds seemed like hours. Tom opening the carriage door freed the moment. He must have rushed alongside the train, looking in the carriages, and eventually found me. I was in a dream. If he had not been there, or had not opened the door, I sometimes feel I might still be there. It was a strange feeling, easily explained away by logic, but nonetheless a lasting impression.

Tom had a taxi waiting. His friends Josh and Betty offered us hospitality, great warmth and tea with toast. As they were married, Josh could live off base. Their happiness was apparent. We too would be sharing such a lifestyle soon. Tom must have worked hard to make the arrangements. He produced a ring card to measure my finger and dashed off to buy the ring. Never had there been such a ring. Bought in a hurry, cheaply, but with more love than anyone could have given, it meant so much.

Meanwhile, I prepared myself for the ceremony. We walked to the Registry Office. I remember only that the room was drab. With Josh and Betty as witnesses, in just a few minutes, with minimum fuss, we said the words which publicly joined Tom English and me, Doris Bigmore, together for ever. The room was transformed by our moment of joy, which I am sure touched all who were present.

After lunch with Josh and Betty, I sat at Tom's feet by a cosy fire; he stroked my hair. We were like a long-married couple.

Tom's friends told me something of their lives. Betty, from Southampton, had met Josh that year at Hamble. It was there that Josh and Tom had become friends. Josh and Betty had met, fallen in love and married quickly. They too had been caught up in the mood of wartime. Josh's family lived in South Africa and communications were becoming difficult. They had not waited for the usual family customs of procedure and ceremony but married at Hamble as soon as was possible. Josh was so happy to live off base and together they faced an uncertain future, at least in a state of love and support for each other.

Towards evening we were alone when Tom broke the news that he must go back to camp. He had booked a room for me at Everards Hotel. The fine building still stands, probably unnoticed by the majority of passers-by, with the ground floor taken up with a pizza restaurant and building societies. I realised that Tom must have made all the arrangements when he did not have leave. In fact, leave was unlikely so he had gone ahead. That evening he was on standby. There was simply no choice; he could not be absent.

And so it was that sadly we spent the first night of married life apart. It was the very last thing that we wanted.

Tom took me to the room. It boasted a huge soft bed and subtle lighting, creating just the right atmosphere for the love that we both longed for, but was our fate to be denied. It was with the greatest of difficulty that Tom left me to accompany his friend back to the last place on earth that he wanted to be.

Left on my own, there was much to reflect upon. I smiled to myself as I contemplated the future. Very importantly, I would resign my post.

Married women teachers were not allowed. It seems unbelievable in these times of equality. But it was a regulation that was not questioned at the time and I saw it as a way to be with Tom much more. He would obtain a small allowance for me and probably gain promotion soon. We would manage and be happy.

We talked of our plans, to include a honeymoon, probably in January.

Tom and his regular RAF colleagues were under a great deal of pressure. They were stretched beyond limits, waiting desperately for new air crews to be trained. They all hung on to the belief that their lives would improve by Christmas. Tom hoped to be given some leave after then.

There must have been thousands of wives and girlfriends who heard the deep fears of their men, many so-called "secrets" hinted at as part of loving relationships. The isolation suffered by men involved in war must be intolerable for the many who are basically quiet and gentle people for whom any kind of aggression is alien.

I spent a strange night of mixed emotion. The whole situation felt dreamlike. But the impact of the day's event, combined with the ring so proudly worn for Tom, reassured me greatly.

The next day, Sunday, I spent time with Josh and Betty. There was no transport home. We began to talk, beginning to lay foundations for a relationship that we expected to continue. I so wished that Tom would appear. He did not.

The next day, I travelled home. Perhaps my biggest concern became the fact that by staying on I had missed a day's work. This caused me much anxiety, although this was tempered by the knowledge that I could now give notice and would be leaving at Christmas. Somehow this certainty gave me some feeling of strength which was welcome, a stable point in a world that seemed to be falling apart. I was ready to leave my work and began to feel ready to face a new life with all its difficulties, as long as Tom and I were together.

It was unreal being back at home. Outwardly nothing appeared different and I resumed my work. Inwardly I only had thoughts for Tom. My colleagues gave me a set of saucepans, the children a table cloth. My parents were rather shocked at the speed of my marriage. They must have been hurt, but there was nothing they could do to change the situation.

As the days wore on I became downhearted. Phyllis and Walter Harrap were a great comfort. With them at least I felt understood, and could be myself. I do not doubt that many people suspected the apparently hasty marriage was as a result of my being pregnant. That was of course untrue.

It became more difficult to remain cheerful and optimistic. As the weeks dragged on I began to experience despair. My sister-in-law had sent a wedding cake and some money as a present. The cake remained untouched. All I desired in the world was to be with Tom. Nothing else mattered.

Just when I most needed news, Tom wrote to say that he had been granted ten days' leave starting on 21 December. He requested that I make some arrangements for our honeymoon. Somehow my emotions had been exhausted. Unable to respond, I put the letter carefully to one side.

A few days later Tom appeared one dark evening. The weather was atrocious, too bad for flying. They were relieved of duties for the night. Tom, who I learned was now flying out of Honington, had borrowed an old motorbike and made the hazardous journey to see me. He was cold and rain-soaked when he knocked at the door. I answered. I recall that my feelings were numb. Poor Tom. He explained how in the few hours' respite from duty there had been no time or means to get to see me. The strain was intolerable for us both. He looked hungry and tired and I realised how desperately unhappy the last few weeks had made me.

We walked to a pub outside town. As we sat sipping rum by a blazing fire, the warmth slowly seeped back into us. I agreed to book our holiday, deciding that the Bull at Halstead would be suitable. We began discussing our plans, the walks we would have. This was to be the marking of the real beginning of our time together.

By the time we parted we both felt happier even though yet another parting was painful. We so needed to be together. I was feeling more isolated than ever, living at home, when in truth my life had moved on. My life was in a kind of limbo, like seaweed washed ashore waiting for the next tide to take it back into the ocean, its real home.

We parted with a gentle embrace. The passion could wait. Tom saluted me and disappeared into the black night, the machine spluttering in protest.

I had been released from a spell of despair. There was much to do, arrangements to make, plans and dreams to fulfil.

We exchanged several letters. Emotions were mixed. Tom's anger about the war came out in this response to his situation.

. . . Had I known you earlier, perhaps I should have read this book sooner. If only you were here now, we could thrash this out. The facts and figures for rearmament, particularly those that concern the RAF, more than justify my own fears that arise from half-knowledge, rumours and duff gen handed out to us. It's terrible how we are sent like lambs to the slaughter. To survive, one has to be cynical. I can't discuss this, here, now, but could have done so last year. How I wish I'd known you then, my dearest. Talking about this book with you would have opened up new possibilities, which I can't explore now.

In another letter, he was bubbling with happiness.

I have an address in Bury St Edmunds for you to visit this coming Saturday. I haven't seen it, but I'm told it's a bungalow on the outskirts. Unless it's absolutely hopeless, take it, dear — from 28th December. We can get settled in and have three days in a place which will be our home. Dearest, I have never longed for leave as I do now. Trust me to love and care for you. I won't rush you. Just to be with you, without interruption from the outside world, will be paradise for me.

The bungalow was just right, even if we would have to share the kitchen and bathroom. I wrote to Tom with enthusiasm:

I paid Mrs Atkinson £2 deposit — on good faith, if you like. We shall be going there after spending

Christmas together. I shall have to ask her if I can move my belongings before we go away. She was very understanding — when I explained that I hadn't any bottom drawer, she said that for the time being I can use her bed linen until I can buy some — dockets will limit me as will money! Really, apart from my books and personal things, I shall have nothing — no trousseau, no bottom drawer. At least I haven't got them to cart around, have I? Isn't it exciting Tom? So much to look forward to!

Your adoring wife,
Doris

I had some Christmas cards printed. This was a luxury I could not really afford, but felt that the occasion warranted it. Very carefully I chose the words: "May Christmas, like a beacon light, shine through the coming year, bring hopes of a just and lasting peace. From Tom and Doris English". I remembered when Tom had said that the prospect of our marriage was to him a beacon light in the darkness of the present. I asked Tom for a list of his friends and relatives and prepared cards for posting.

So far I had heard nothing from his parents. As I addressed the envelope to them, I wondered whether they were unhappy about the marriage. If they were, at least Tom was not at home to witness or suffer their hostility. It was nearing the season of goodwill and, although there was little sign of that in the world, I felt that members of a family should be at peace with each other.

Tom received my letter confirming our honeymoon booking at a time of fear and anxiety for him. Some of his friends had failed to return from a raid over the Heligoland area. They had again gone out in daylight, in flights of three. Certain that his flight would soon be briefed for one of these raids, he was unable to share my pleasure.

Tom must have feared that his Christmas leave was at risk. The intensity of bombing raids over the enemy was increasing. There was no sign of new crews. Tom wrote to our dear friends the Harraps. He told them of his frustration at our being apart. He admitted that he hated the war, he was angry that our lives were out of our control. Poor Tom, he was so brave to express his fears in that way. He must have been so utterly lonely. The Harraps understood his fears and were saddened by the letter.

He wrote to me.

Dearest One,

I'm glad we're "us", darling. I'm so thankful you are you, the only person who exists for me. Doris, my own, adorable wife, keep the same always. I will shower you with love, faith and strength until the end of the world — into Eternity.

As ever,

Your very own Tom.

The sentiments expressed in that letter cannot in my mind be matched by anyone else. They never have been.

All the preparations were complete. I only had to wait a few more days, for Tom and me to be together.

Our attention was drawn increasingly to the war. It now looked as though hostilities were sure to continue beyond Christmas. Gradually, we all had to accept the awful truth that until then had seemed impossible. Even though I was married to an airman and knew something of what was really happening, our quiet and rural life continued almost in defiance of world events. Reports about air raids still seemed not to affect us personally. Tom had talked about friends who had not come home from bombing raids. Still it did not truly impinge on my life.

Before Christmas we sat at home listening to Lord Haw Haw on the radio. At that time we were more fascinated than believing of these propaganda broadcasts. They went something like:

Germany calling. Germany calling.
Today, your bombers came over Heligoland and Wilhelmshaven, looking for our navy. But we were waiting there with our fighters. They came out of the clouds and we shot them down like flies.

A chill swept over me. I remembered Tom's words of anger, how they were supposed to fly at night not in daylight. He knew the German radar could detect them, and in daylight their vulnerability was in no doubt. "Sitting targets, Doris, that's what we are."
Tom's words echoed in my mind.

We had both read *England Speaks Again* by Phillip Gibbs. His writing took the form of an informed debate. He argued that war was unwanted by the vast majority of people, but looked for by those who sensed that gains were likely, for instance manufacturers of arms. His views made little difference to events, but caused

Tom to question his situation. He also knew that having been trained by the RAF and given his solemn commitment to his country, there was nothing that he could do to change his situation.

These thoughts caused him intense frustration and only made him more aware of what he now stood to lose. Everything.

CHAPTER
ELEVEN

The Eighteenth of December

A few days after our wedding Tom took part in a reconnaissance mission over the North Sea. Years later I read the details from the RAF *Operations Record Book*. He flew in one of a number of Wellington 1A aircraft (No. 2939) with five airmen aboard. The record shows that they took off in groups about 14.00 returning at 18.05. All aircraft had landed by 18.30. The remarks reported that "Apart from fishing vessels off the coast of Yarmouth, no shipping of any description was sighted. Visibility throughout that patrol was very poor, and heavy rain was encountered in patches. The reconnaissance was carried out without opposition."

On 18 December, No. 9 Squadron had been standing by for coastal duties. Nine Wellington Mark 1A aircraft were ready armed with No. 5 series bombs.

At 9 a.m. on 18 December 1939 they took off in broad daylight; the wind was light, the sky reported as overcast with cloud at between 1,000 and 2,000 feet. Visibility was quite good at 2-4 miles.

As the planes approached the coast of Europe they were quickly spotted by German radar. It was said that because it was quite unexpected that they were flying in daylight they were at first mistaken for flights of geese, especially as they flew in similar formation.

But when it was realised that they were planes flying in clear view it was a relatively easy task to attack first.

German reports said, "We shot them down like flies."

The records show that at 17.30 two Wellingtons landed, one at North Coates, the other at Sutton Bridge, with two crew reported wounded. Previously at 16.00 two aircraft landed at base. It seems they were the only crews to survive unscathed.

The complete crews of the five remaining planes were listed as "reported on Casualty Signal as Missing".

Later, four members of a five-man crew were picked up from the North Sea. They were taken to Grimsby Hospital, but I did not know at the time and never received news.

Tom was lost, along with his whole crew of six men.

So many of Tom's friends were lost on that day that there was no one left to tell me what had happened. I never saw or heard from Josh again.

It was to be some weeks before the news came officially. In the confusion of the times our marriage had not yet been registered with the air force.

Eventually, all the bureaucracy was put in order, an easy task compared with the prospect of mending broken hearts and picking up pieces of broken lives.

Tom English had met me just in time to achieve the one thing he desired most before flying to a wasteful death in the service of his country.

Grenadier

The Queen she sent to look for me,
The sergeant he did say,
"Young man, a soldier will you be
For thirteen pence a day?"

For thirteen pence a day did I
Take off the things I wore,
And I have marched to where I live,
And I shall march no more.

My mouth is dry, my shirt is wet,
My blood runs all away,
So now I shall not die in debt
For thirteen pence a day.

Tomorrow after new young men
The sergeant he must see,
For things will be over then
Between the Queen and me.

A.E. Housman

If Christ should walk this earth again,
Traverse once more the ways of peace —
Would His work be all in vain?
Or lust and greed of man decrease?

His presence near would shame a few
Instil with fear the hearts of most,
But Saxon, Aryan, Negroid, Jew,
Would strive to bring His former ghost.

They would not look for peace — these fools!
Peace spells doom to their wilful way,
Blindly keep to their set rules
Of hate, injustice, and dismay.

Tom English, 1939

Life's Elusiveness

Upon a peak extremely high,
His aims were such to do or die,
He set about a course to take,
Opposed by life, to make or break;
The journey grim he struggled through,
Exhaustion great but courage true,
To find the peak beneath his feet
One peak of many to defeat.

Tom English, 1939

ISIS publish a wide range of books in large print, from fiction to biography. A full list of titles is available free of charge from the address below. Alternatively, contact your local library for details of their collection of ISIS large print books.

Details of ISIS complete and unabridged audio books are also available.

Any suggestions for books you would like to see in large print or audio are always welcome.

ISIS

7 Centremead
Osney Mead
Oxford OX2 0ES
(01865) 250333

1	21	41	61	81	101	121	141	161	181
2	22	42	62	82	102	122	142	162	182
3	23	43	63	83	103	123	143	163	183
4	24	44	64	84	104	124	144	164	184
5	25	45	65	85	105	125	(145)	165	185
6	26	46	66	86	106	126	146	166	186
7	27	47	(67)	87	107	127	147	167	187
8	28	48	68	88	108	128	148	168	188
9	29	49	69	89	109	129	149	169	189
10	30	50	70	90	(110)	130	150	170	190
11	31	51	(71)	91	111	131	151	171	191
12	32	52	72	92	112	132	152	172	192
13	33	53	73	93	113	(133)	153	173	193
14	34	54	74	94	114	134	154	174	194
15	35	55	75	95	115	135	155	175	195
16	36	56	76	96	116	136	156	176	196
17	37	57	77	97	117	137	157	(177)	197
18	38	58	78	98	118	138	158	178	198
19	39	59	79	99	119	139	159	179	199
20	40	60	80	100	120	140	160	180	200

201	211	221	231	241	251	261	271	281	291
202	212	222	232	242	252	262	272	282	292
203	213	223	233	243	253	263	273	283	293
204	214	224	234	244	254	264	274	284	294
205	215	225	235	245	255	265	275	285	295
206	216	226	236	246	256	266	276	286	296
207	217	227	237	247	257	267	277	287	297
208	218	228	238	248	258	268	278	288	298
209	219	229	239	249	259	269	279	289	299
210	220	230	240	250	260	270	280	290	300

301	310	319	328	337	346
302	311	320	329	338	347
303	312	321	330	339	348
304	313	322	331	340	349
305	314	323	332	341	350
306	315	324	333	342	
307	316	325	334	343	
308	317	326	335	344	
309	318	327	336	345	